THE POWER TO BEGIN

UNLOCK YOUR MOTIVATION AND EMBRACE YOUR GOALS

BY

CHARDINEY JACKSON

The Power To Begin

Copyright © 2026: Chardiney Jackson

All rights reserved. No part of this publication may be produced, distributed, or transmitted in any form or by any means, including photocopying, recording, or other electronic or mechanical methods, without the prior written permission of the publisher, except in the case of brief quotations embodied in critical reviews and certain other non-commercial uses permitted by copyright law.

Published by Conscious Dreams Publishing
www.consciousdreamspublishing.com

Book Journey Mentor: Daniella Blechner
Editor: Parris Rohoblt and Elise Abram
Typesetting and eBook Formatting: Amit Dey

ISBN: 978-1-917584-78-4

Dedication

For my daughter, Amara.
May you grow brave, courageous, and confident in your ability to begin again and again.

And to those who believed in me before I fully believed in myself—thank you for shaping who I am today and who I am still becoming.

Contents

Introduction

Hello there, my very special reader. I am so glad you picked up this book. This tells me something important about you already—you want more. More clarity. More energy. More confidence to start, and the resilience to keep going.

I've spent more than ten years helping people unlock their potential, whether in classrooms, coaching sessions, or conversations that spark growth. My reason for writing this book is that my expertise comes from having been where you are, staring at a goal, a dream, or a challenge, wondering if I had what it took to keep moving forward. Motivation isn't something you wait for; it's something you build, strengthen, and revive. And that's what this journey is about.

This book is for you if you've ever:

- started something with excitement, only to lose momentum halfway
- felt stuck in a cycle of I'll-do-it-tomorrow
- wanted to make progress but weren't sure where to begin
- faced setbacks that left you questioning whether it was worth trying again

If any of that sounds familiar, you're in the right place.

Think of this book as your personal toolkit for a journey to reach your next big goal: your compass, your oars, your sails to take you across the unpredictable sea called Life.

Inside, you'll find practical strategies, reflective exercises, and encouragement designed to help you:

- understand what truly drives you
- break through the barriers that keep you stuck
- find and sustain your motivation over the long haul
- renew your energy when life knocks the wind out of your sails
- build a toolkit you can return to whenever you need a boost

Here's how I want you to approach this: don't just read it—use it. Pause when something clicks. Journal your thoughts. Try the exercises. Come back to the parts that feel especially relevant when you need them. This isn't about perfection; it's about progress.

So, let's begin together. Think of me as your coach on this journey, someone in your corner reminding you that you already have what it takes. You just need the tools and the mindset to unlock it.

So, let's get started!

Chapter 1: Understanding Motivation

Discover how we are all pushed forward.

Have you ever felt super excited about a new goal only to lose steam and interest after a few weeks? Maybe you've struggled to get started on something critically important, even though you *really* wanted to begin? You're not alone.

Everything I've accomplished since starting college has felt at first like winning the lottery—exciting and full of possibility—only to fade with time, growing stale like forgotten leftovers in the fridge. Motivation can feel unpredictable. It fills you up when inspiration strikes and vanishes when things get tough. What if you could learn not only how to create that push, but how to sustain it as well?

Motivation isn't just a random spark out of nowhere; it's something we can actually understand, nurture, and strengthen. Developing this skill has taken some time. As each new goal appeared, the journey demanded hard work and perseverance, but I never stopped daring to pursue something bold again. In this chapter, we'll explore what drives us, why we sometimes lose motivation, and how we can tap into the right kind of motivation to stay committed.

Why Motivation Matters

Motivation is the fuel that propels every action we take. It's what pushes us to chase our dreams of degrees and promotions, show up for responsibilities like motherhood and marriage, and ultimately grow into the truest, best versions of ourselves. But here's the key: not all motivation comes to us the same way. To truly harness its power to the absolute fullest, we need to understand how it works.

The Psychology of Motivation: Why We Do What We Do

Scientists and psychologists have studied motivation for decades, uncovering powerful insights about what keeps us going as people. Let's break down a few key theories that help explain why motivation works … and sometimes doesn't, beginning with American psychologist Abraham Maslow.

Maslow's Hierarchy of Needs: The Ladder of Motivation

Think of motivation like climbing a ladder. Abraham Maslow's famous theory (1943) suggests that we need to meet certain basic needs before we can focus on higher goals. The ladder would look something like this:

1. **Basic needs (food, water, safety):** If you're struggling to figure out your next meal, pay your bills, or get enough sleep, it's tough to focus on big dreams. If the roof over your head is unstable, then you might feel like you have bigger problems than passing your college course to earn

a degree. I personally had moments in my childhood that were extremely tough, like no-electricity-in-the-apartment tough, a circumstance not conducive to earning good grades. I now know that obstacles to fulfilling your physiological needs require giving yourself a lot of grace regarding having and sustaining ambition.

2. **Belonging and Love:** When you're supported by friends, family, or mentors, it becomes easier to stay focused and energized, but when that sense of connection is missing or strained, motivation can feel heavier, like you're carrying everything on your own. I've experienced both sides of that. I'm deeply grateful for the community I have now, but before I was married, when my dating life was chaotic, it was incredibly hard to stay motivated. Training for my military fitness test or practicing my national pageant opening dance routine felt twice as challenging when my relationship life was draining instead of uplifting. In those seasons, I had to lean on my parents and best friend for grounding and encouragement. Their support reminded me that motivation isn't just an internal spark; it's strengthened by the people who stand with you.

3. **Esteem and Achievement:** Once we feel secure and supported, we crave a sense of accomplishment. Feeling centered and self-assured is a superpower that makes you unshakable or extremely vulnerable, depending on the season you're in. That inner critic can sabotage your

hopes and dreams from the inside, and quickly! Holding tightly on to the gift of optimism is something I have always found in my mother, and it has helped me keep my head held high many times. Feeling fulfilled in your safety and community can take you to the moon. For those who feel secure but might be struggling with love, remember to find confidence in yourself. Look at everything you've overcome and be proud, knowing you have the strength to achieve even more.

4. **Self-actualization:** This is the tip of the ladder, where we pursue personal growth, purpose, and fulfillment. Discovering your fullest potential is life-changing, and feeling close to it is amazing. This peak takes time and a lot of lessons learned, so don't rush it if you haven't gotten there yet. Being delayed never means being denied. As a wife, a mother, a senior leader in the military, and in my civilian life, it has taken a lot of experiences for me to feel well-rounded. I have been tried and tested, and I've succeeded and failed, so to still see myself smiling in the mirror day after day is a blessing. I'm connecting the dots of work I'm good at, advice I can share, and love I can give, both to others and to myself. I know my triggers and good and bad habits, and I can predict risks and know the consequences very well. Life is a gift of ups and downs, but after a while, we all realize that the journey gives us so much wisdom. You will never avoid facing another storm once one is over. Become resilient and good at damage control, and you will be all right.

If you've ever felt unmotivated despite having big goals, it might be because something lower on the ladder needs attention first, and that's okay. But now you know why, and you know that you're not alone in this diminishing and flooding of motivation.

Self-Determination Theory: The Three Sources of Motivation

Think of your motivation like a fire, one that can burn brightly when it's fed the right fuel. Two researchers, Deci and Ryan (2000), spent decades exploring a simple but powerful question: what truly drives people to act, grow, and thrive? Their work revealed that motivation strengthens when three core psychological needs are met:

- **Autonomy:** feeling free to make your own choices
- **Competence:** believing you have what it takes to succeed
- **Relatedness:** feeling connected to others and supported in your journey

These needs aren't luxuries; they're the building blocks of lasting motivation.

When we feel stuck or unmotivated, it's often because one of these three elements is missing. If we don't feel in control of our goals, if we doubt our abilities or feel isolated, motivation can fade fast. The good news? We can always adjust our approach to rebuild it. I was highly motivated and committed as I trained for my first half-marathon as it was my personal goal. Then, for over two months, my ankles continued to swell, and I later found out that I was having a bad reaction to my high blood pressure medication. I felt frustrated and powerless. Even though I still wanted to train, my body wasn't cooperating. It no longer felt like I was in control of my progress; my sense of autonomy was gone, and I nearly gave up.

In high school, I gave up so much because I did not have the confidence I needed to succeed. I was deathly afraid of being judged and denied. I jumped ship on trying out for the band after weeks of preparing for flag-girl routines. I practiced with the lovely modeling club but literally ran out of line during auditions before they could even call my name to attempt a model walk. Cheerleading, I thought, would be different, but nope. I practiced a few routines before I stopped showing up, denying anyone the chance to deny me. It wasn't until I went to college that I began to believe I was capable of more, and I now know it's because I built a community, and that gave me confidence. I went on to do TV anchoring, win Homecoming Queen, tackle cheerleading (made it to tryouts and on the team), and hold various student leadership positions. My proudest achievement was an internship with U.S. Senator Tom Carper—how blessed I was when things were aligned! Sometimes, life does things on its own timeline, and that's okay. It's never too late for a comeback.

Expectancy-Value Theory: Do You Believe You Can Succeed?

This theory is simple but powerful. According to Eccles and Wigfield (2002), we're more likely to stay motivated if we believe our efforts will pay off and we value the outcome.

For example, if you're training for a marathon but doubt you'll ever be able to run ten miles, your motivation might fizzle. If you trust that consistent training will get you there, and you truly value the accomplishment, you're far more likely to push through the hard days.

Achieving over a decade in the United States Air Force was possible because of the advice my father gave me before I ever took the oath. As a Special Operations Marine veteran, he told me, "Join the Air Force. They'll look out for you, help you balance family life, and make the journey to retirement more manageable than other branches. You'll have the support you need to succeed and thrive." He planted this seed in my mind from day 1. Long-term was the game plan, so when tough times came every couple of years, I remembered his words. It was like eating a can of spinach, and I was Popeye. For those too young to understand that reference, it gave me courage, strength, and vision, and allowed me to remain dedicated to the path for 20 years.

Intrinsic vs. Extrinsic Motivation: Which One Lasts?

Motivation comes in two forms, according to Deci and Ryan (1985):

- **Intrinsic motivation:** This comes from within. You do something because it genuinely excites or fulfills you. For example, you wake up early to paint simply because you love it. Ever since my daughter could eat solid food, I've made it a point to slice up fresh strawberries for her lunch. I still remember her very first day at daycare, carefully adding strawberries to her meal, hoping to send her a little comfort from home. Now, every week, I pick up a carton of fresh strawberries just for her, and at five years old, she still delights in them. Of course, I know they're healthy, but—if I'm honest—I keep going that extra mile because it makes me feel like a good mom to give her something she loves. Even on my busiest days, taking a few moments to pack that little Ziplock bag of berries brings me real happiness. It's a small ritual that has become my own personal fulfillment, and I imagine I'll keep doing it until the day she insists she's had enough. Though even then, I'll probably try to remind her how much she's always loved strawberries.
- **Extrinsic Motivation:** This comes from external rewards: you do something because you'll get something in return.

For example, waking up early to get to work because you want to obtain a promotion. This can be tough when we have to go to battle with our good ole friend, *emotions*. At times, you have to find the energy to be committed to your long-term goal, believing you'll succeed even if you can't see the reward or feel doubtful that you'll truly obtain it. Earning a master's degree as an adult, while working a full-time corporate job and attending in-person classes one hour away was tough. I remember nights when I had an upcoming fitness test in the Air Force Reserves and was going to the gym to train after my class. The schedule was work, drive to class, engage in class, drive an hour home, work out, and be in bed by 11 p.m. At times, you question if it's worth it, but I have had two careers for over a decade and obtained my master's degree part-time in four years, so you can do it if you really want that return on your investment. It's your time; make it valuable!

Both types matter, but research shows that intrinsic motivation leads to deeper, longer-lasting commitment. When we do things because they align with our passions and values, we don't have to force ourselves—we want to do them because they are true to us and who we are. It's not easy to aspire to be a good mom, but it's in my heart to work hard to achieve it. Obtaining my degree and working hard in my career are difficult commitments—I'm not going to lie: being a good mommy is more genuine.

This is why finding a way to connect your goals to something that is meaningful to you is crucial. If you're struggling with motivation, ask yourself:

- Do I actually enjoy this?
- Can I find a way to make it more meaningful?
- What deeper purpose does this serve in my life?
- Can I identify a personal core value that aligns what I do with who I am?

Your Motivation Matters

Motivation isn't just about willpower. It's about understanding yourself. When you know *why* you're motivated (or why you're not), you can make real changes that help you stay on track. Not being honest with yourself will become a repeated theme in your life with severe consequences if you don't call it out. Be in denial that you're imperfect if you want; it will only hurt *you* the most in the end. So, take the time to truly reflect, analyze, and dig down. I journal when something seems off with me, and I know I have goals, but I am just not making progress. It is okay if you don't start strong or if you fall off after doing really well. Successful people learn from their mistakes, so take the time to make a good plan for recovery and see tomorrow as a truly new day, one with truly *new* possibilities!

In the next chapter, we'll dive into some of the biggest barriers that get in the way of motivation and how you can push past them. Once you understand what's stopping you, you can take back control and start moving forward.

You have the power to begin. Let's do this.

Chapter 2: Address Common Barriers to Motivation

Break the waves and push past the obstacles ahead.

So, you're feeling good now after some better insight into motivation. You understand how it works and why it matters, but let's be honest, understanding motivation is not sufficient. Sometimes, even when we *want* to take action, something gets in the way. Maybe it's procrastination. Maybe it's self-doubt. Maybe it's just that nagging feeling of being overwhelmed. For me, being overwhelmed leads to procrastination, like analysis paralysis, if you've ever heard of that. It's a psychological state where you're so overwhelmed by thinking, options, or the fear of making the wrong choice that you can't make a decision at all.

Whatever it is for you, know that you're not alone. Every single person, no matter how disciplined or successful they are, faces motivational roadblocks. Want to hear the good news for you? No matter where you fall, all barriers can be broken down, somehow, someway. In this chapter, we'll identify the most common obstacles holding us back and, more importantly, how to push past them, confidently kick them down, or take a big, brave leap right over them.

Barrier #1: "I Just Don't Feel Motivated"

Let's start with the big one: waiting to *feel* motivated.

So many of us fall into the trap of thinking motivation has to *come first* before we can act. We assume we need to *feel* inspired before we can start writing that book, going to the gym, or launching that business.

Here's the truth: *Motivation follows action, not the other way around. You have to bust a move!*

Think about the last time you didn't want to do something, like clean your house or exercise. But once you started, you really got into it. That's because taking action, even in the smallest way, creates momentum.

I used to start my mornings thinking *I didn't sleep much*, or *I slept terribly*, and I'd let that set the tone for my whole day. Then, one day, my husband—who I admire deeply—said, "Do you think I get perfect sleep every night, and I still give 110 percent?" That hit me hard. I realized I was putting my progress on pause simply because my day hadn't started out perfectly.

Once I dropped that mindset, everything shifted. I became more productive because I treated every morning as a fresh opportunity, regardless of how I'd slept or how motivated I felt in the moment. Now, I'm even more driven to show up for the goals I worked toward the day before. We owe it to ourselves to keep going, especially when every small step counts.

You can't always control how you feel when you wake up, but you *can* control how you show up. Lead with your mind, and your body will follow.

The Fix: The 5-Minute Rule

If you're struggling to get started, tell yourself: *just do it for five minutes.*

- If you don't feel like working out, commit to just **five minutes** of movement.
- If you're avoiding a tough project, set a timer for **five minutes** and start working on it.
- If you're dreading writing that book, start with **one sentence**.

Chances are, once you begin, you'll want to keep going. And even if you don't, five minutes is still better than zero minutes. I've found this great for tough projects at work. It's like once I begin, I get locked in and productive, which allows me to get curious and creative. But if I get overwhelmed, it's okay. I at least got started, and I can take a break. I love scheduling working blocks on my work calendar to ensure it's in my face, and I chip away at projects in advance of the delivery date. I do the same in my personal calendar. In my cell phone, I set up work blocks for certain items to progress toward a goal. Motivation comes and goes, but you have to rip the band-aid off to feel the fresh air and wake up!

Successful people move because they have to. Taking care of your business and opportunities to better yourself is the best push you can give yourself.

Barrier #2: Feeling Overwhelmed About Beginning—"I Don't Know Where to Start"

Have you ever looked at a really big goal and felt instantly paralyzed? The dream seems so huge, so far away, that you don't even know where to begin, so you don't. Your inner critic instantly screams, "Are you nuts? Back away slowly before someone holds you accountable, okay?"

This is one of the biggest killers of motivation: our brains naturally resist overwhelming tasks because they seem too complex, too exhausting, or too risky. Specifically, the amygdala is your brain's emotional alarm system. It helps detect danger and prepares you to respond, often before you're even consciously aware of it. As the brain's threat-detection center, it processes complex information and uncertain situations such as threats, triggering avoidance responses like fight, flight, or freeze. Neuroscience supports the idea that perceived complexity and risk can trigger a fear or stress response, leading to avoidance (LeDoux, 1996).

The Fix: Break It Down

Instead of focusing on the big goal, shrink it into tiny, manageable steps.

- Want to write a book? Forget about the whole thing; just outline *one* chapter.
- Trying to get into shape? Don't worry about losing 20 pounds; just take a ten-minute walk *today*.
- Starting a new career? Don't stress about the whole journey; just *update* your resume.

The key is progress, not perfection. Every small step forward is still movement. I love creating a plan with short, intentional steps that lead to a big goal. One step alone will not land you your dream internship or promotion, but a series of focused actions can move you closer.

When I set my sights on a vice president role, I could not guarantee the outcome, but I could claim the goal and take control of what was mine to own. I identified the exact role I wanted, mapped out the skills it required, earned my coaching certification, and intentionally built the right relationships. The path from Senior Associate to VP was not smooth. My manager at the time did not speak highly of me, but I stayed committed to showing up, doing the work, and making sure no one could deny my effort or readiness.

In the end, my hustle and consistency outshone the negativity, and the hiring manager saw my potential. I did not control the politics, but I did control my preparation and persistence. That is what made the difference. When you commit to what is within your control, especially when the odds feel stacked against you, you build real momentum. One day, you will look back, proud that you never cut corners.

When Will Smith was eleven, his father tore down the brick wall in front of his shop and challenged Will and his younger brother to rebuild it by hand, one brick at a time. At first, the task felt overwhelming and impossible, but together, brick by brick and day after day, they kept working. In time, the wall was complete.

Years later, Will reflected on the lesson. "You don't set out to build a wall. You say, 'I'm going to lay this brick as perfectly as I can.' You do that every day, and soon you have a wall" (2021).

Barrier #3: Fear of Failure—"What If I Mess Up?"

Let's be honest: sometimes, we avoid things, not because we're lazy, but because we're afraid. What if we try and fail? What if we look foolish? What if we're not as good as we thought? Disappoint myself, disappoint others—it's a mortifying thought!

This fear keeps so many people stuck, but here's something powerful to remember:

Failure isn't the opposite of success—it's part of it.

Think of someone you admire: a great athlete, an entrepreneur, a CEO, a music artist, a politician, an activist, or a leader within your community. Even if it's your amazing mother or father you look up to, every single one of them has failed, probably a lot. Way more than you realize. But guess what? They kept going with their eyes on the prize!

I was a first-generation college student, and while my parents were very proud and supportive, we were all very unprepared. I'll never forget arriving on campus, and all three of us were shocked that we had to pay for textbooks; that's how new it all was to us. My academic advisor incorrectly placed me in a 300-level math course as a freshman, and I quickly felt like I didn't belong because *I did not* have advanced skills. Because I mentally checked out and stopped attending class, I earned a lovely F. That class haunted my GPA for years, and though I re-enrolled as a senior, the damage, emotionally, academically, and financially, stuck with me.

Despite the embarrassment that haunted me, I kept going. I honestly feared messing up again, especially when I started graduate school. Most people don't know that before completing my master's in Communications in 2022, I actually started two other programs, one in Educational Leadership (thinking I might become a principal) and another in Business (thinking I needed an MBA to succeed in corporate).

The truth is, I stumbled a lot, but I didn't give up. Every misstep helped me learn more about who I was and what I really wanted, and over time, I stopped doubting and started believing I could do better, and I did.

The Fix: Reframe Failure

Instead of seeing failure as the end, see it as data. It's feedback that teaches you what doesn't work so you can analyze, adjust, and keep moving forward.

- Didn't hit your fitness goal? Figure out what needs tweaking and go back at it.
- Bombed that presentation? Learn from it and crush the next one.
- Launched a business that didn't take off? Take the lessons learned and move forward. Most successful entrepreneurs fail *multiple* times before succeeding.

The key is to stop seeing failure as a reflection of *who you are* and start seeing it as *a necessary step to growth.* It is never personal; it's inevitable. But you can conquer it and come out successful in the end.

Barrier #4: Lack of Confidence—"I'm Not Good Enough"

Self-doubt is a dream killer. If you don't believe in yourself, it's terribly hard to take action.

Self-confidence isn't something you wait for; it's something you have to *intentionally* build.

The Fix: Focus on Small Wins

Confidence grows when you prove to yourself that you can do things. Forget about proving anything to other people. That has neither substance nor sustainability. Collect the small wins for yourself:

- If you're nervous about public speaking, start with small meetings or events.
- If you want to write but don't think you're good enough, start journaling daily.
- If you doubt your ability to lead, take on a small leadership role in your community.

The more small risks you take, the more you prove to yourself that you *can* handle challenges. You can be uncomfortable and survive, maybe even thrive, which builds real, unshakable confidence.

At my going-away party for Air Force basic training, I stood there in heels, a cute dress, and long, curled hair, looking fabulous but feeling terrified inside. My cousin, who's in the Army (and whom I adore), joked, "Uhh, you do know where you're going, right?" I laughed and responded with confidence, but the truth was I had no idea what I was walking into.

Still, I wasn't trying to prove anything to her. I needed to prove something to *myself*. I come from a proud line of service: my dad's a Marine, my Pop Pop served in the Army, FBI, and as a police officer, and my great-great uncle was a Tuskegee Airman.

Their legacy lit a fire in me. It wasn't what I originally planned after college, but it was a solid opportunity to grow, lead, and invest in my future.

I was 23 when I joined, and my recruiter warned me that if I gained even one more pound, I'd be ineligible for basic training. That pressure was real, but I pushed past it. Thirteen years later, I'm still serving.

I didn't feel ready. I didn't feel "enough." But I took the leap anyway. It was a decision that changed my life. The confidence came *after* the risk, not before. I want anyone reading this to know that if you feel like you're not good enough, take the step anyway. Growth comes from doing.

Barrier #5: Distractions—"I Just Can't Focus"

Between adulting through daily responsibilities, a little social media fun, emails coming and going, all our notifications, and everyday life crises, staying focused in today's age is harder than ever. Because we're constantly distracted virtually and in real life, our motivation takes a major hit.

The Fix: Control Your Environment

You don't have to rely on willpower alone. Instead, try setting up the environment around you for success:

- **Eliminate distractions:** Put your phone in another room while working or set your phone on Do Not Disturb mode to instantly reduce interruptions for 10–15 minutes.

- **Set a dedicated time:** Block off focused time on your calendar and set an actual timer to execute a task, including time to think/reflect/analyze, and not just meetings for preparation and action.
- **Use the "Two-Minute Rule":** If a task takes less than two minutes, do it immediately to prevent procrastination. Knock it out!
- **Build a focus playlist:** Certain sound environments can boost concentration and quiet mental noise. Use your favorite music app to gather four or five tracks that calm and center you, like water sounds, smooth jazz, or soft instrumentals.

Your environment should *support* your goals, not work against them. You control that. Find things that you can control and never lose yourself in the things you cannot change.

Then, honestly, some days, friend, there is just too much going on, and that is okay. I have been there. As a mom, I have had plenty of nights where I had a full plan ready to go, only for Amara to wake up sick, not sleep well, or sleep in unusually late. Every parent knows that is a red flag.

Suddenly, she is staying home, and my entire day shifts. No meetings. No workout. No prep for that important call with the Executive Director I was trying to connect with to sponsor my journey to Vice President.

Now, it's all about checking the medicine cabinet, figuring out her current weight for the right dose, and deciding if I'm working from home or not working at all.

On days like that, I've learned to pivot, re-prioritize, and remind myself, "Delayed doesn't mean denied."

I might not stick to my original seven-day plan, but that doesn't mean I should throw it away. Maybe it will become next month's plan because, right now, hand, foot, and mouth has other ideas.

I've learned to be flexible because I'm serious about making progress. If you *can* eliminate distractions, *do it*, but if you *can't* right now, give yourself grace—you can still win, even if it takes a little longer.

Final Thoughts: Motivation is in Your Hands

Motivation is not something you find. It is something you create, brick by brick. This reminds me of my marriage and my commitment to staying motivated to be a good wife. It is not easy, and it is not instant. No one enters a marriage without needing to grow, change, self-assess, struggle, fail, and make mistakes.

With the right partner, though, you become a better version of yourself. That is how motivation works too. Like any meaningful goal, it is built brick by brick, effort by effort, reflection by reflection, moving you closer to the outcome you want.

I am grateful that my husband shares this perspective and level of commitment. Together, we work toward milestones, whether that is a ten-year anniversary or a twenty-year one, knowing that consistency and intention are what truly sustain the journey.

In any area of life, just like in marriage, once you understand what's blocking you, you can *move it* and take back control. Reflect on the last big achievement you've had, and if it feels too far in the past, friend, you *owe* it to yourself to make the next win happen. You deserve it. No more keeping your head in the past. Tomorrow is a brand-new day full of limitless possibilities. Can you change your mindset enough to get *out* of your own way?

What's one barrier that's been holding you back? How has it been keeping you from making progress? Decide on one small step you can take today to push past the block. Anything is better than absolutely nothing. Any progress, no matter how small, is *way* better than none.

Ultimately, if the day is just too heavy for you, here's one of the best pieces of advice my mom gave me: "Just go to bed." Seriously. When the day is falling apart, don't try to force it—sleep it off, let tomorrow come quicker, and boom! You've got a fresh start. Maybe you'll get some much-needed rest, wake up with a little more peace, clarity, and energy, and be ready to face what's next.

Because, no matter where you are right now, you have the power to begin or the power to go to bed (unless your kid is sick, then you do not have the power to do either, sorry).

As we continue on to **Chapter 3**, we'll dive into practical techniques to not only find motivation but also sustain it for the long haul. Get ready to take action!

Chapter 3: Techniques for Finding and Sustaining Motivation

Catching the wind and finding your rhythm.

At this point, you know how motivation works **(Chapter 1)** and what might be blocking you **(Chapter 2),** but how do you actually create and sustain motivation in your daily life?

Let's be honest, motivation isn't something that magically appears and stays forever. It comes and goes like waves. Some days, you're energized and ready to tackle your goals. Other days, you'd rather binge-watch your favorite show in bed and avoid everything. *Bridgerton* and I were untouchable when I didn't feel like being productive. I'd practice my British accent and eat warm, freshly baked chocolate chip-lovers cookies made from frozen cookie dough, wrapped snug as a bug in a rug in my favorite king-sized blanket.

That's normal. The secret to success isn't always feeling motivated. It's knowing how to keep going even when you're not. Not being motivated is a frequent occurrence while goal-chasing!

In this chapter, we'll cover practical techniques to not only *find* motivation but *maintain* it for the long haul.

Step 1: Get Clear on Your "Why"

Think about a time when you felt truly and deeply motivated. Chances are, you were not chasing a random goal. You were connected to a *meaningful, purpose-filled reason* behind it.

Your "*why*" is your personal motivation that fuels you from head to toe. It's what keeps you going when things get tough because they always get tough; we can depend on that.

How to Find Your "Why":

- **Ask yourself:** *Why is this goal important to me?*
- **Dig deeper:** When you answer, ask *why* again. Repeat until you hit a true reason that lives within your core.
- **Make it personal:** Your "why" should excite *you and* fill you up with purpose not something you think you "should" do, or that someone else wants you to do.

Example*:* Instead of saying, "I want to get fit," dig deeper.

→ *Why?* "Because I want to be healthier."

→ *Why?* "Because I want to have more energy to keep up with my kids."

→ *Why?* "Because I want to be the kind of parent who is active, present, and sets a good example as an active role model."

That's a strong "*why.*" When you connect your goal to something deeply personal, it's much easier to stay committed, especially during hard times, when you will be tested and tempted to quit.

My "Why":

I joined the Air Force Reserves at 23 because I wanted more for myself and my family: stability, growth, and purpose. After graduating from college, living back at home, and earning just enough from a part-time job, I realized I needed to take charge of my future. I wanted financial independence, access to healthcare, and the ability to provide support to my family when the time came.

But beyond the practical reasons, I craved discipline, resilience, and long-term health. I saw the military's physical requirements as a commitment to staying fit for life. And once I joined, I realized I had signed up for much more than I'd expected: sacrifice, transformation, and a test of my mental strength.

Balancing military duties, a civilian career, graduate school, fitness standards, and personal sacrifices wasn't easy. There were many times I questioned whether I could keep going, missing family events, juggling two careers, and feeling like I had to prove my commitment in both worlds. But every time it got demanding I came back to my "why": I chose this path to grow, to serve, to build a life of purpose and resilience. That fire still fuels me.

Step 2: Use the Power of Habit

Motivation is great, but you can't rely on it *alone*. The real secret to successful goal execution? *Turning motivation into habits.*

Once something becomes a habit, you don't have to rely on willpower to do it; you just do it. Thankfully, the body will follow the mind.

How to Build Motivation-Boosting Habits:

1. **Start small:** Instead of setting an overwhelming goal, shrink it down. (Example: Instead of "meditate for 30 minutes," start with two minutes.)

2. **Attach it to an existing habit:** Link your new habit to something you already do. (Example: After making your bed, do ten push-ups.)

3. **Make it easy:** Remove any possible conflicts or complications and implement proactive steps. (Example: If you want to work out, lay out your clothes the night before. If you want to read more, keep a book by your bed.)

4. **Track your progress:** Seeing progress keeps motivation high. (Example: Use a habit tracker, journal, or simple checklist. Whether it's on your phone or in a physical notebook, it's all helpful.) Observing your differences is key!

Example: Instead of saying, "I need to write a book," make it a daily habit—*"Every morning after coffee, I'll write 200 words."*

It is undeniable that small daily actions repeated over time lead to massive results. Consistency will take you to where you want to be.

My Story: Building Habits That Carried Me Across the Finish Line

Training for my first half-marathon in 2024 meant I couldn't just "try" to make time—I had to build habits that made time. Life was *full*: I was working full time, serving in the military, being a mom and a wife, yet I committed to running 13.1 miles by November 9.

I started small, training in January and setting monthly milestones. Each Sunday, I'd sit down and plan my week: When could I run? Morning? Lunch break? Evening? Some weeks were messy and uncomfortable: I ran in the rain, in the heat, after long days, in makeup, jeopardizing my skin health, on the treadmill, in the quick windows before school pickup. Some weeks, I ran back-to-back days just to stay on track.

I didn't always feel motivated, but I made it a habit. My Sunday run-planning became non-negotiable. I tracked my runs and looked back often. It reminded me how far I'd come and boosted my confidence to keep going.

No one trained with me or ran with me on race day, but the habits I built carried me through. I didn't need willpower every time; I just followed the plan I'd made. This just-do-what-you-can-when-you-can mindset got me across the finish line.

Step 3: Set Yourself Up for Success with the Right Environment

Your environment influences your behavior more than you think. If your space is full of distractions and temptations, it's incredibly difficult to stay on track.

How to Create a Motivation-Boosting Environment:

- **Remove distractions:** Keep your phone out of reach when working.
- **Surround yourself with inspiration:** Design a personal vision board, set reminders of your goals, or follow people who inspire you.
- **Make success easy:** If you want to eat healthier, keep healthy snacks visible and available. If you want to work out, put your gym shoes by the door.
- **Find an accountability partner:** Have someone to check in with who can help boost commitment.

Example: If you want to wake up earlier, put your alarm clock across the room.

Set up the environment around you so that motivation becomes automatic.

My Story: Designing an Environment That Fuels My Dreams

My bedroom isn't just where I sleep; it's where my vision lives. I've created a vision board that reflects every area of my life: personal, professional, financial, and health goals. It's packed with words, images, and even photos of myself to remind me of where I've been and where I'm going.

It's not about perfection; it's about growth. Seeing that board every morning and night gives me direction, hope, and purpose. It's a daily visual reminder that I'm a dreamer, I'm going places, and I owe it to myself to take one step closer every day.

I even keep a photo of it on my phone and share it often, not just for motivation but for accountability. Having it in my most personal space is intentional: my environment reflects my mindset, and my mindset is set on greatness.

Step 4: Use the "Two-Minute Rule" to Beat Procrastination

We often lose motivation because tasks feel overwhelming. The *Two-Minute Rule* solves this by making the first step ridiculously easy.

How It Works:

- If something feels too big, shrink it down to a two-minute version of the task.
- Once you start, momentum often takes over, and you'll want to keep going.

Example:

- Instead of "Go for a five-mile run," say, "Put on my running shoes."
- Instead of "Clean the whole house," say, "Wipe down one countertop."

Action creates momentum. The absolute hardest part is just starting, so make starting easy for yourself.

My 90-Day Pageant Hustle

While I was looking for ways to speak and inspire in my community as a motivational speaker, I heard about a local pageant through my volunteer work on the Delaware United Way Young Professionals board. I figured, "Why not?"

I entered, did what I loved, and luckily, I won!

What I didn't realize? Winning the Ms. Delaware title meant I had to compete at the national level in Tampa, FL., in just 90 days, on my own dime, without guidance, without sponsors, and with no real clue where to start.

It felt huge, but instead of freaking out or quitting, I took the first small step. I wrote myself a sponsorship letter, printed a few copies, and walked into a local business, a large chain restaurant, asking to speak to the manager so I could pitch for support.

That one step led to another. The manager just about laughed in my face, looking me up and down in my pageant heels and crown. Still, it gave me the courage to think, "Well, that sucked. Let's see if the next place will be better."

Before I knew it, I had won some people over. They believed in me. And after three months, I had raised almost $7,000 through incredible local sponsors and GoFundMe, enough to cover my travel, my wardrobe, and all the unexpected pageant fees.

I took that same one-small-step approach with everything: training a little each day, eating better, planning my travel and how I'd show up as my best self. By the time I stepped on that stage, people couldn't believe the transformation from April to July, and I won first runner-up in my first national pageant!

It wasn't magic; it was momentum. Each small step gave me more confidence to take the next. This experience is why I believe so deeply in just starting, even if it's messy, even if it's tiny. You don't need a perfect plan, just a first step.

Step 5: Reward Yourself for Progress

Our brains love rewards. When you celebrate small wins, you reinforce motivation and make it much easier on yourself to stay on track.

Ways to Reward Yourself:

- **Immediate rewards:** Treat yourself to something small after completing a task (a nice coffee, a quick break, a favorite song).
- **Milestone rewards:** Celebrate big achievements with something meaningful (a new book, a fun experience, or a self-care day).
- **Internal rewards:** Sometimes, just acknowledging your own progress can be enough. Keep a "wins" journal and write down your small successes.

Example: If you're trying to build a daily reading habit, allow yourself to enjoy a small treat *only* once you've completed your reading goal.

Training your brain to associate positive reinforcement with progress keeps your motivation strong.

Why I Reward Myself (and You Should, Too)

Training for my half-marathon meant staying motivated for months, through cold, rain, boredom, and days when even my Beyoncé playlist couldn't save me. So, I made a deal with myself: If I trained three days a week for a month, I'd buy new running shoes. Next month? New workout gear. It became a fun game: show up, work hard, then treat myself. Those little rewards gave me the boost I needed when discipline alone wasn't enough.

But rewarding myself isn't just for workouts: I celebrate career wins, new degrees, and especially birthdays, with or without a party. That tradition started in college, when I was away from home, and my mom told me I didn't need anyone to take me out or go with me. I could simply go to my favorite restaurant and order whatever I wanted, so I did. Alone. And I loved it—no people-pleasing, just me, my good food, and my joy.

Since then, I've made it a tradition to celebrate myself, sometimes big, sometimes small. For my 28th birthday, I had a photoshoot. For my 34th, I enjoyed a quiet morning at Starbucks with a warmed-up blueberry muffin and a notebook to reflect and dream. Big or small, every celebration honors the effort I've put in and the progress I've made.

The point is, don't wait for someone else to clap for you—celebrate your wins, however they come. Just don't overdo it. Save rewards for real effort, but never let your achievements go unnoticed, especially by you.

Step 6: Keep Motivation Fresh by Revisiting Your Goals

Even the best motivation techniques can fade if you never check in on your goals. Periodically checking in is important for achieving success. That's why *regular reflection* is key.

How to Stay Aligned with Your Motivation:

- **Do weekly check-ins:** Ask yourself: Am I still excited about this goal? Do I need to adjust anything?
- **Revisit your "why":** If motivation dips, reconnect with why you started.
- **Adjust when needed:** It's perfectly okay to shift your approach if something honestly isn't working.

Example: Set aside five to ten minutes every Sunday to reflect on your progress and make any necessary tweaks.

Motivation is not, and never will be, about perfection; it's about progress. Checking in helps keep you continuing on the right path that is true to your definition of success.

Why I'm a Proud Planner Girl

I'm a *big* planner girl, the kind who feels genuine joy opening a fresh planner every January. My sister, Symone, and I even have a tradition: every year, we compare which planners we're about to "entrust our lives to." We'll spend an entire Saturday afternoon chatting like kids about the sizes, colors, layouts, and features that perfectly match our intentions for the year ahead.

In 2024, I even gifted my favorite work girlfriends with planners for Christmas. Yes, it runs that deep! For me, planning isn't just about stationery; it's about *strategy*. I'm a visionary who thrives on structure. Being prepared, organizing my thoughts, and mapping my path to success isn't optional. It's an annual non-negotiable.

But here's the truth: planners aren't about being perfect. They're about being prepared. I use mine to set goals, break them down by month, week, and day, and, most importantly, check in with myself regularly. After the first quarter, I like to pause and ask: Am I still aligned? Has something shifted? Do I need to pivot? These moments of reflection keep me both hopeful and grounded.

Even if I don't accomplish everything, I always feel proud of the progress I've made. One goal achieved out of ten is still one step closer to where I want to be, and that's something worth celebrating.

Planning helps me balance it all—military life, family, career, and "me time"—without losing sight of what matters most. You don't have to chase perfection. Just give yourself the space to pause, reflect, and adjust. That's how you stay connected to your *why*, and how you keep showing up for yourself, one page at a time.

Final Thoughts: Motivation Is a Skill, Not a Feeling

Motivation isn't something you *wait* for; it's something you *build*.

By using these techniques, you can find motivation when you need it and sustain it long enough to reach your biggest goals.

What's One Technique You Can Start Using Today?

Pick one and put it into action. Because the truth is, friend, you don't need to feel ready; you just need to begin.

In **Chapter 4,** we'll explore what to do when motivation runs out and how to renew it when you hit a slump.

Chapter 4: Strategies for Renewing Motivation

Find the strength to catch your second wind.

Let's be real: staying motivated *all the time* is never realistic.

Even the most successful, most disciplined people lose motivation. They feel stuck. They hit incredible roadblocks. They have horribly difficult days where they just don't feel like doing anything.

The difference? *They don't wait for motivation to magically return; they aggressively renew it.*

That's what this chapter is all about: how to refresh your mindset, reignite your energy, and get back on track when motivation starts to slip.

Step 1: Recognize the Signs of a Motivation Slump

Before we can fix a motivation dip, we need to recognize when it's happening.

Common Signs of a Motivation Drop:

- You procrastinate more than usual.
- You feel mentally drained or uninspired.
- You start questioning your goal: *Is this even worth it?*

- You make excuses for not taking action.
- You feel overwhelmed and don't know where to start.

If any of this sounds familiar, don't panic. A *slump doesn't mean failure. It just means that you're human, and it's time to reset, and that's okay.*

Big Dreams, Low Battery

I've always been wildly ambitious. One little spark of an idea, and suddenly I'm planning a new business, a really cool podcast, three new certifications I really need, possibly a PhD, and a TED Talk, too. All before lunch.

But every once in a while, I'll notice a shift. The ideas still come—fast and loud—but my energy doesn't always follow. I'll get excited, then stall. Sit there. Question everything. Open a new tab. Get overwhelmed. Close all tabs.

I used to push through that feeling, tell myself I was just being lazy or distracted, but over time, I've realized it's not a flaw. It's a signal from my soul.

When I start avoiding next steps or saying, "I don't feel like it," more than usual, it usually means I'm not being lazy; I'm tired. Mentally, emotionally, and sometimes physically. And that's when I know it's time to pause everything.

I have to listen to my body, slow down, and take care of the basics: sleep, food, sunlight, moving my limbs, and seeing people I love.

It sounds simple (and honestly kind of boring), but pulling back from the hustle is what clears the fog. That's where the motivation starts to come back, not from doing more, but from doing what matters at a pace that feels human and sustainable.

Turns out, hitting pause isn't failure; it's maintenance, and ambitious people need that more than anyone. Don't feel bad, my friend!

Step 2: Reconnect with Your "Why"

When motivation fades, one of the best ways to get it back is to remind yourself *why* you started your journey in the first place.

How to Reignite Your Purpose:

- **Revisit your original goal:** What excited you about it? What impact will it have on your life?
- **Visualize the outcome:** Imagine yourself achieving your goal. How will it feel at the finish line?
- **Write a letter to yourself:** Remind your future self why this goal matters to you.

Example: If you've lost the motivation to exercise, remind yourself: *I started this because I want to be stronger, have more energy, and feel confident in my body. This isn't just about fitness; it's about my overall well-being.*

When your "why" is front and center, it's easier to push through the tough moments. You have to be strategic to be successful; you can't, unfortunately, skip the hard parts, but you can make it.

I Got the Promotion, Then Asked, "Now What?"

At the time of writing this, I'm 35, with a pretty full résumé. I'm an Associate Director of Learning and Development, a former Vice President at a top global investment bank, and a Sergeant in the Air Force Reserves for more than thirteen years. So, yeah, I've been busy.

This year, obtaining the role of Associate Director was a step closer to my dream of becoming a Chief Learning Officer. To take it, I walked away from over a decade of corporate life. The VP title was great on paper, but unfortunately … Let's just say that my work-life balance had me living out of my suitcase more than my home dresser.

As excited as I was to level up, I also had a moment of "Wait … what now?" I had gotten what I'd asked for, so why did I feel a little lost?

That was when I hit pause and wrote a letter to myself, a reminder of *why this role matters* in the big picture. I told myself, *You can't take your foot off the gas now. This is part of the plan.*

I also visualized myself ten years from now, sitting in the Chief Learning Officer seat, confident, impactful, and aligned with my purpose. That mental image became a compass.

Because here's the thing: even high performers question themselves. *Confidence needs maintenance.* And leadership? It's not about having all the answers—it's about keeping the vision alive, even when it gets a little foggy.

Sometimes, reconnecting with your "why" is what steadies the wheel. You don't have to feel 100 percent sure every day, but you do have to keep showing up, especially when your purpose is bigger than your fear.

Step 3: Change Up Your Routine

Sometimes, a loss of motivation happens simply because things feel stale. If you're bored, your brain tunes out and is tempted to turn off.

How to Add Fresh Energy to Your Goals:

- **Change your environment:** Work in a different space, rearrange your desk, or try a new gym.
- **Try a new approach:** If your workouts feel repetitive, try a new activity. If your work routine is draining, shake it up.
- **Incorporate fun:** Find ways to make the process more enjoyable (music, friendly competition, or rewarding yourself).
- **Switch your schedule:** If you're always working on your goal at the same time of day, and it's not working, experiment with a different time of day.

Example: If writing has become a struggle, try writing in a coffee shop instead of at home, or switch from typing to handwriting. A small shift can make a tremendous difference.

Tiny Changes, Big Energy

When I need a boost, I make a new playlist. It's one of my favorite ways to shake up my energy. Over the years, I've made workout mixes filled with Beyoncé when I'm feeling powerful, Jay-Z when I'm focused, or a lineup of female rappers when I need hyped-up energy. Recently, I made a T-Pain playlist that somehow included Chingy and listen, I've never smiled so hard after two miles with two more to go. It takes me right thurr, back to that 2003 music video. Music shifts your mindset, and sometimes, that's exactly what you need.

Changing things up has always helped me reconnect with my motivation, especially during hard seasons.

Back in fall 2021, I was finishing my master's degree *during COVID, with a newborn.* (Yes, I know—let's all take a deep breath together.)

Everything about my routine had to change. I didn't want to be away from my baby, and with all the chaos in the world, we were glued to each other at home, so I adapted.

I'd read during her naps, write papers while sitting next to her, and steal moments whenever I could focus. Sometimes, she'd yank a printed article out of my hand and try to eat it, and honestly, it was adorable. Exhausting, but adorable.

What surprised me most was that I *didn't* want to save my work for when she wasn't around. I wanted her to see me doing it. I wanted her to feel part of the journey, even if that meant pausing every ten minutes to protect my flashcards from drool.

I also have a habit of buying myself fresh flowers in the weeks I feel like I need them. It sounds small, but it made working from home feel less like *just* home. After a long weekend of family life and busyness, the flowers remind me that the space is also mine, and I deserve to feel good in it.

Sure, I was still tempted to fold laundry or start dinner instead of focusing endlessly on work, but those little acts of self-care—the music, the flowers, the flexibility—helped me show up with more joy and motivation.

I realized something big: *it's my job to give myself what I need to stay inspired, not anyone else's.*

Sometimes a change of scenery, a new vibe, or a cute bouquet is the difference between burnout and breakthrough.

Step 4: Lean on Accountability & Support

When motivation begins to fade, one of the best ways to get back on track is to involve others. Otherwise, it can be a very lonely journey.

Ways to Use Accountability to Your Advantage:

- **Find an accountability partner:** Find someone to check in on your progress.
- **Join a group or community:** Being surrounded by like-minded people keeps you inspired.
- **Make it public:** Announce your goal to friends, family, or social media for extra commitment.
- **Hire a coach or mentor:** Sometimes, expert guidance can reignite your drive.

Example: If you're struggling to stick to a workout routine, find a workout buddy who won't let you skip a session. If you need motivation to write, join a writing group that holds you accountable.

When others expect you to show up, you're far more likely to stay committed. It is never a perfect guarantee, but it does more good than harm for you to gain support.

Your Goals Need Witnesses (Even If It's Just You)

I could throw on my coach's hat and tell you to call me for a pep talk—and I *mean* that—but, seriously, let's talk accountability.

Try this:

You can either tell *everyone*—your mailman, the barista, the person at the self-checkout—and let that good energy fuel you, *or* you can work quietly and lean on someone who sees you without needing a performance. Because that's what accountability really is: someone who helps you keep going, whether you're sprinting or crawling.

Now, doing a half-marathon once? Wild.

Doing it again next year? That's a special kind of delusion … which I fully signed up for, apparently.

For me, lately, the person who keeps me accountable is my Auntie Cherie.

Even though my Aunt lives in a different state, we text, we vent, and we send screenshots of our runs (and sometimes our excuses). She reminds me I'm not crazy for chasing big goals while being a wife, a mom, working two jobs, and somehow trying to run miles in between a five-year-old melting down over her morning outfits, texting friends back a week later, and email alerts chiming into the weekend and evening hours.

Her encouragement, honesty, and little you've-got-this notes help drown out my inner critic.

Because, let's be real, chasing big dreams alone? That's a heavy lift. Motivation fades fast when it's just you versus your own brain.

But here's the thing: *if you don't have an Auntie Cherie, be your own Auntie Cherie.*

Leave yourself notes. Be kind in your self-talk. Set reminders to celebrate progress, not just results.

Support doesn't always show up as a person right away, but if you stay open, creative, and willing to look, it will come.

Until then? You can absolutely be that support system for yourself.

Don't give up on finding your people. Not looking is more harmful than not having. There are local clubs, groups, chapters, associations, mentors, partners, and even apps that can help. It starts with making the decision that you don't want to do this alone.

You don't have to be loud about your goals; you just have to stay committed to them. With help.

Step 5: Take a Break (Yes, Really!)

Sometimes, a moment lacking motivation isn't a sign that you're lazy. It's honestly a sign that you're *burned out!*

Signs You Might Need a Break:

- You're constantly exhausted, even after rest.
- You feel resentful toward your goal instead of excited.
- Your creativity or focus has completely disappeared.
- You're experiencing stress or frustration more than experiencing progress.

How to Reset Without Losing Momentum:

- **Step away briefly:** Take a short break (a weekend off, a social media detox, a change in routine).
- **Engage in self-care:** Rest, relax, and recharge your energy (*time*: 15 minutes, an hour, just engage in something that fills your cup).
- **Give yourself permission to pause:** Sometimes, resting for a few days helps you return stronger. It works for the body when working out, as well as the mind.

Example: If you're feeling drained from your side business, schedule a weekend with zero work. Focus on hobbies, sleep, or spending time with loved ones. You'll come back refreshed.

Rest Isn't a Luxury—It's a Strategy

When I need to fill my cup, I don't need a luxury spa or a flight to Bali. I need a couch, some California sushi, and my handsome husband. Sometimes we watch a movie, sometimes I just join him in laughing at whatever random YouTube video he's enjoying on a Tuesday night. And honestly? That small, simple time together makes me feel present again, like I'm living my life, not just racing through it.

Because let's be real, chasing your dreams can get lonely. You start to feel resentful of people who seem to have time for fun, naps, or hobbies. Meanwhile, you're juggling goals like flaming swords.

Another great reset for me? Quality time with my Pop Pop. Being around someone who's known me my whole life reminds me of who I am, not just who I'm trying to become. That kind of connection is grounding. It brings me back to the version of me that doesn't need fixing or upgrading, just love.

And look, breaks don't have to be fancy: I love a hot bath with eucalyptus-scented bubbles. I believe in taking PTO just to stay in mismatched pajamas, binge-watch *Game of Thrones* (again), and try a new Pinterest recipe. I almost never skip a nail or hair appointment—especially the ones I've been putting off for three months—because, at some point, you have to stop rescheduling and say, "I deserve this." Lately, I've found peace just walking outside in the sun for 15 minutes between meetings, doing absolutely nothing.

Now earlier, I mentioned that sometimes you'll have sleepless nights, but you still have to give 110 percent. That's true—sometimes—but I want to be clear: pushing through exhaustion should be the exception, not the expectation. Seven nights of just-getting-by isn't sustainable. You're not a machine, so please don't treat yourself like one.

Perseverance is powerful but so is *intentionally planning your rest*. Rest can't be something you hope happens. It has to be something you protect. Even the most successful people don't always get eight hours, but they do eventually make time to recharge because they understand that sustainability matters more than speed.

Yes, caffeine and energy drinks in moderation can help, but a daily dependence on them will catch up to you. Be cautious and care for your body; it's the engine that gets you to every finish line.

You don't have to earn your rest; you just have to recognize when you need it.

If you're not sure, do a quick check-in: Are you exhausted? Irritable? Hiding from your calendar? Yeah, it's probably time.

Rest isn't weakness; it's wisdom. It's how you avoid burnout, bitterness, and breakdowns.

I don't guilt-trip myself when I need self-care or time with family, which took practice but is now a habit I protect. Because when I come back from a break, no matter how small, I feel better, clearer, and ready to conquer again.

So give yourself permission to take a break. Be creative. Be kind. Have non-productive fun.

Your future self will thank you.

Step 6: Recommit with a Fresh Start

When your motivation fades, sometimes the smartest move is to call it a night: go to bed, let your mind rest, and give yourself permission to begin the next day with a clean slate. A fresh start means releasing yesterday's frustration, forgiving the bad choices, the mistakes, your regrets, and choosing to show up again with renewed energy, optimism, and intention. There is nothing wrong with returning to square one. What matters is that you're willing to begin again. You owe it to yourself, friend. You deserve the success that lies on the other side of starting again.

How to Create a New Motivation Boost:

- **Set a new short-term goal:** If the big goal feels far away, focus on a smaller milestone.
- **Restart as if it's Day 1:** Pretend you're just starting again. Bring back the excitement!
- **Track progress in a new way:** Try a journal, an app, or a new method or system to keep things interesting. Try a new notebook or sticky notes. Colored gel pens have been my latest fascination when writing down my progress this year.
- **Celebrate how far you've come:** Instead of focusing on what's left, look at how much progress you've already

made. The world is a crazy place, and if you wait for others to celebrate you first, it can make you miserable. So step up and treat yourself well by recognizing the effort you've given. It deserves to be acknowledged!

Example: If you've been struggling to stay consistent with a project, set a Fresh Start Monday, when you treat it like a brand-new challenge. Restart with new energy and a new plan. Same ol' goal, but with a fresh, new perspective, leaving behind your fear, frustrations, or failures. Mondays are great for feeling like you have new possibilities to plan and execute.

Creating a New Motivation Boost

One of my first big dreams came to me during the fall of my junior year in college. Graduation was quickly approaching, and even though I was about to become a first-generation college graduate—a dream I was proud of—I didn't know what I wanted to do next.

I had a mentor at Wesley College who was a pilot at the local Air Force base. He often encouraged me when I felt anxious about the future. His example, combined with my family's legacy of service, inspired me to pursue a new goal: becoming a United States Air Force officer.

I reached out to a recruiter and, during our first conversation, he mentioned that strong letters of recommendation—specifically from local politicians—could make my application stand out. I didn't know any politicians, but that became my new short-term goal. I googled to find local leaders, emailed several of them, and introduced myself, sharing my pursuit and attaching my résumé.

I heard nothing back until Senator Tom Carper's office called, not to offer a letter, but a spring internship. They said, "Complete the internship, and we'll gladly write you one."

That opportunity changed everything. It reminded me that when motivation fades or obstacles appear, you can always find new energy by creating a smaller, fresh goal that moves you forward.

I could've been discouraged and given up, but instead, I pivoted, and that pivot opened a door I never expected. Sometimes the best way to stay motivated is to start again with a fresh goal and trust that it will lead you somewhere even better.

Final Thoughts: Slumps Are Normal. What Matters Is What You Do Next

Losing motivation doesn't mean you've failed; it just means you're human.

People who succeed? They don't let the slumps stop them. They recognize the dip, the change in their pace, the shift in their energy, and determine that it's time for a reset.

If your motivation has been slipping lately, take a nice, deep breath: you have *not* lost your drive; you simply need to *renew it.*

You have the power to begin again and again.

Here is where the journey continues into **Chapter 5**, where we'll build your ultimate Motivation Toolkit, so you'll always have strategies in your pocket to keep moving forward.

Chapter 5: The Motivation Toolkit

Strategies to steer toward success.

By now, you've learned:

- What motivation is and how it works (*Chapter 1*)
- What blocks motivation and how to overcome it (*Chapter 2*)
- How to find and sustain motivation (*Chapter 3*)
- How to renew motivation when it fades (*Chapter 4*)

Now, it's time to put everything together in your personal **Motivation Toolkit**, a collection of strategies you can use any time you need a boost.

Let's be real. Life is unpredictable, and your motivation will naturally ebb and flow, but with the right tools, you can keep moving forward, no matter what comes your way.

Tool #1: The "Why" Reminder

Your "why" is your most powerful motivator, but over time, it's easy to lose sight of it.

How to Use It:

- Write down your "why" in a place you'll see it daily (like a mirror in your bedroom or bathroom).

- Record a video or voice memo reminding yourself why this goal matters.
- Create a physical or virtual vision board with images, words, and phrases that inspire you.

Example: If your goal is to run a marathon, put a sticky note on your mirror that says, "I'm doing this to prove to myself that I can."

Tool #2: The Five-Minute Rule

When you don't feel like doing something, just commit to five minutes. This small step often creates the momentum and energy to keep going.

How to Use It:

- Set a timer for five minutes and start the task.
- If you still don't feel like continuing, stop, but most of the time, you'll want to keep going.

Example: Struggling to start a workout? Just put on your shoes and stretch for five minutes. You'll likely end up feeling like you want to do more, which will ultimately lead to you doing more.

Tool #3: The Two-Minute Rule

If a task feels overwhelming, break it into a *two-minute action*. This tricks your brain into getting started.

How to Use It:

- Instead of "Work out for an hour," say, "Do ten squats."
- Instead of "Revamp your résumé," say, "Update one bullet point."
- Instead of "Organize the closet," say, "Sort five items."

Example: If you don't feel like journaling, just write one sentence. That's it. Starting is the absolute hardest part of any task and any goal. When you do, you'll likely keep going.

Tool #4: The Habit Stack

Motivation is incredibly unreliable. But *habits* create true consistency.

How to Use It:

- Attach a new habit to an existing habit.
- Say: "After I drink my water with breakfast, I'll take my vitamins."

- Say: "After I check my morning emails, I'll review my top three priorities for the day."

Example: If you want to practice daily self-care and deep breathing, attach it to something automatic: After I park my car at work, I'll take three slow, intentional breaths before going inside (even if I'm running late).

Tool #5: The "Gamify It" Trick

Making tasks feel like a *game* can increase your motivation.

How to Use It:

- Set up a reward system (e.g., treat yourself to sushi or a yummy snack after completing a hard task).
- Compete with yourself (try to beat yesterday's effort—do better than you did 24 hours ago).
- Use an app or a tracker to measure progress (checklists, habit trackers, etc.).

Example: If you want to save money, turn it into a challenge: Can I commit to two whole weeks of no spending?

Tool #6: The "Accountability Partner" Hack

We are more likely to stay motivated when someone else is watching. Nobody likes to be a disappointment or to be proven a liar. We all want to be seen as inspirations, role models, or upcoming success stories.

How to Use It:

- Find a goal buddy, someone who will check in on your progress.
- Join a community: surround yourself with like-minded people.
- Make it public: announce your goal to friends or social media.

Example: If you struggle to wake up early, text a friend every morning when you're up. Knowing that they expect your message will push you to get out of bed.

Tool #7: The "Change Your Environment" Shift

Sometimes, motivation fades because our surroundings feel stale. A small shift can refresh your energy. Be honest with yourself, because the impact can be tremendous!

How to Use It:

- Work in a new space: try a coffee shop, library, or a different room at home or in your office space.
- Declutter your workspace: a clean space boosts focus —time for a refresh!
- Add visual cues: place motivational quotes where you'll see them (on your computer, on your desk, your notebook, etc.).

Example: If you're feeling stuck in your workout routine, switch to outdoor runs instead of the treadmill. A simple change can make all the difference in your continuing the journey.

Tool #8: The "Energy Check" Reset

Lack of motivation is often a sign of low energy, not laziness. If you can't get it together, you need a reset, and that's okay.

How to Use It:

- Get enough sleep—motivation is impossible when you're exhausted.
- Move your body. Even a short walk can boost energy.

- Eat well. Junk food leads to energy crashes, so this is not just for a healthy body but also a strong mind to do the things you dream of doing.

Example: If you're struggling to focus, ask yourself: Am I tired, dehydrated, or just mentally drained? A quick break or (healthy) snack might be all you need.

Tool #9: The "Celebrate Small Wins" Method

Celebrating progress keeps motivation high. *It's the small wins that build momentum.*

How to Use It:

- Keep a "wins" journal. Write one thing you've accomplished each day (big or small).
- Share your wins with someone. Get excited about progress. (This can be anyone, but you have to share.)
- Treat yourself when you hit milestones; rewards reinforce good habits. (Again, big or small, *you* be the judge!)

Example: "If your goal is to go back to school for a certificate or degree, celebrate the moment you're accepted. Completing the application, gathering paperwork, and navigating logistics takes real effort. That acceptance is proof you showed up for yourself. Starting is half the battle—and you've already begun."

Tool #10: The "Permission to Rest" Rule

Pushing *too* hard will lead to burnout. Sometimes, the best way to regain motivation is to *take a break.*

How to Use It:

- Schedule rest days—taking a break is part of all progress.
- Do something fun: play, relax, engage in hobbies, or connect with friends/family.
- Step back, then restart. A short reset can help you return stronger.

Example: If you're feeling drained from a big project, take a full day away from it. You'll come back refreshed and more motivated.

Final Thoughts: Your Motivation Toolkit Is Ready

Motivation isn't about luck; it's about having the right tools for the right time.

Now you have everything you need to stay motivated, even when life gets busy, obstacles arise, or energy dips.

Whenever you feel stuck, come back to this toolkit, pick a strategy, apply it, and keep moving forward.

At the end of the day, motivation isn't about feeling ready: it's about taking action, even when you don't feel like it ... especially when you don't feel like it!

And remember ...

You ALWAYS have the power to begin, again and again and again. You never have to quit!

What's Next?

You've made it to the end of this book, but this is just the beginning of your journey.

- Pick one tool from this chapter and apply it ... *today*.
- Revisit your goals and refresh your motivation.
- Keep taking small steps: progress always beats perfection.

Remember, this book isn't meant to be read just once. It's a *resource* you can come back to whenever you need to regroup, refocus, or reignite your motivation. Each time you revisit it, you'll see something new, something that speaks to where you are in that moment.

Remind yourself often: *This journey will have roadblocks, failures, and mistakes, but that's okay.* You're human. Each day is a new chance to start again, to try things differently, and to keep moving forward. Don't be embarrassed by where you are or too critical of how long it's taking. Growth takes time, and every small step matters.

Be gentle with yourself, and trust that you have what it takes to keep going. Your journey starts now, because *you have the power to begin*.

Good luck! Your future self is already saying, "Thank you."

Congratulations! You've Completed The Power to Begin!

Final Thoughts: Your Next Step Begins Now

You now have the tools, strategies, and—most importantly—recognition that you hold the *power to begin.*

But here's the truth: Staying motivated isn't always easy. Life gets busy, challenges arise, and sometimes we need *support* to stay on track.

You might be wondering what a coaching conversation looks like. It's very different from a chat with a friend or family member. As your coach, I serve as an unbiased third party, someone who listens deeply, holds space for your thoughts, and intentionally sets aside my own opinions, experiences, and assumptions.

Coaching is a passion of mine because it helps people believe in themselves, think critically, and unlock transformation that leads to true growth. I use skills such as active listening, asking powerful questions, and what my good friend Kwanzaa King calls "delaying my brilliance," so yours has the room to shine and rise.

My goal is to create a safe, judgment-free space where you can be vulnerable, unpack your inner critic and, more importantly, reconnect with your wisest, most confident self to rediscover your purpose. While I am not a therapist, this book is meant to be a permanent fixture in your journey, offering guidance and encouragement whenever you need it.

If you're ready to take your motivation to the next level, I'd love to help.

Let's Work Together

As an **ICF-Certified Coach, Leadership Expert**, and **Learning and Development Strategist**, I help individuals and teams unlock their potential, stay motivated, and achieve their biggest career goals.

Through personalized coaching, we can work together to:

- break through motivation roadblocks
- create a clear, action-driven plan for your goals
- build an elevator pitch that articulates who you are, what you've done, and where you're going
- hold you accountable and keep you moving forward to success

Whether you're looking to take the next step for growth in your *career or particularly in leadership,* I'd love to support you on your journey.

How to Get Started

* **Schedule a discovery call:** let's chat about your goals and see how I can help.
* **Connect with me online:** follow me on LinkedIn and Instagram (@EliteLeadersCC) for ongoing motivation and insights.
* **Stay inspired:** join my newsletter for tips, strategies, and motivation boosts.

You've already taken the first step by reading this book. Let's take the next one … together.

***Visit EliteLeadersCC.com to learn more and book a consultation session.**

About the Author

Chardiney Jackson, MA, ACC is an author, leadership development strategist, and executive coach passionate about helping people unlock motivation, clarity, and forward momentum in their lives and careers. With more than a decade of experience developing leaders across corporate, higher education, and military environments, she brings a practical, human-centred approach to goal setting and personal growth.

Chardiney currently serves as Associate Director of Learning & Development at the University of Delaware and is the CEO and Founder of Elite Leaders Coaching and Consulting. She is also a Training Manager in the U.S. Air Force Reserves, where she has proudly served for over 13 years. A former Vice President and leadership facilitator at JPMorgan Chase, Chardiney has facilitated leadership development programs nationally and internationally.

She holds a master's degree in Communications, is an ICF-certified executive coach, an award-winning facilitator, and a trusted voice on motivation, leadership readiness, and purposeful growth. Through her writing, Chardiney empowers readers to begin—right where they are—and move forward with confidence and intention.

Acknowledgments

This book would not exist without the support, encouragement, and belief of the many beautiful souls that walked alongside me through this journey.

To my husband, Frederick—thank you for pushing me to share my voice and my truth unapologetically, even when it felt uncomfortable.

To my editor, Parris—your heartfelt guidance helped me turn my thoughts into something clear, powerful, and meaningful.

To Elise, thank you for your kindness, attention to detail, and the care you took in helping strengthen my words. I'm deeply grateful for the time and thought you poured into this work.

And to Danni, thank you for your publishing support. I'm grateful we were able to connect and work together throughout this process.

To my sister, Symone, who listens to me every day with an open heart and an open mind—thank you for protecting my bright light through anything and everything.

To Char, my Wesley College bestie– thank you for your encouragement, insight, and steady belief, which strengthened every word.

To my mentee, Thu—your generosity, perspective, and willingness to grow made this book even more impactful.

To my family and friends—thank you for your patience, love, and constant reminders to keep going, especially on the days when the path felt uncertain and chaotic. As a woman balancing many responsibilities, your encouragement carried me to the finish line more than you know.

To the mentors, leaders, and coaches who challenged my thinking and pushed me to grow—thank you for helping me see possibility where I once saw obstacles and roadblocks. Your guidance shaped not only this book, but the confident, strategic woman I continue to become.

To every coaching client, colleague, and learner from my career journey—thank you for trusting me with your stories and growth. Your courage inspired these pages, and the wisdom shared within them. This work is better because of you, and I am honored by the safe spaces we created together.

And finally, to every reader who picks up this book—thank you for choosing to begin. I hope these words meet you exactly where you are and encourage you to take your next step with confidence.

References

Deci, E. L., & Ryan, R. M. (2000). The "what" and "why" of goal pursuits: Human needs and the self-determination of behavior. *Psychological Inquiry, 11*(4), 227–268.

Eccles, J. S., & Wigfield, A. (2002). Motivational beliefs, values, and goals. *Annual Review of Psychology, 53*, 109–132.

LeDoux, J. (1996). *The emotional brain: The mysterious underpinnings of emotional life*. New York: Simon & Schuster.

Maslow, A. H. (1943). A theory of human motivation. *Psychological Review, 50*(4), 370–396.

Ryan, R. M., & Deci, E. L. (2000). Intrinsic and extrinsic motivations: Classic definitions and new directions. *Contemporary Educational Psychology, 25*(1), 54–67.

Smith, W., & Manson, M. (2021). *Will.* Penguin Press.

Transforming diverse writers
into successful published authors

www.consciousdreamspublishing.com

authors@consciousdreamspublishing.com

Let's connect

www.ingramcontent.com/pod-product-compliance
Ingram Content Group UK Ltd.
Pitfield, Milton Keynes, MK11 3LW, UK
UKHW040021200726
13854UKWH00001B/292

9 781917 584784